Elsie
Weaver

D1470140

Elsie
Weaver

FEBRUARY PATTERNS, PROJECTS & PLANS

by
Imogene Forte

Incentive Publications, Inc.
Nashville, Tennessee

Illustrated by Marta Johnson
Cover by Susan Eaddy
Edited by Sally Sharpe

ISBN 0-86530-130-1

Copyright © 1990 by Incentive Publications, Inc., Nashville, TN. All rights reserved. Permission is hereby granted to the purchaser of one copy of FEBRUARY PATTERNS, PROJECTS & PLANS to reproduce, in sufficient quantities to meet yearly classroom needs, pages bearing the following statement: © 1990 by Incentive Publications, Inc., Nashville, TN.

Table of Contents

PREFACE

February – a month of red hearts and paper valentines

FEBRUARY...

... A TIME of seasonal expectation — Groundhog Day is anxiously awaited by everyone...more snow and ice will extend the days of winter, or the winter thaw will begin, bringing warm winds and the promise of an early spring.

... A TIME of friendship and love — children make valentines for friends and loved ones; secret admirers send special greetings; red hearts and chocolates abound; and children look forward to delicious treats and fun parties!

... A TIME of special days filled with learning — children learn about the history of the nation as they celebrate Washington's and Lincoln's birthdays; awareness of another culture is gained as children learn about the Chinese New Year; proper dental hygiene is reinforced with the observance of National Children's Dental Health Week; and children learn good health habits as they study the human heart and body in accordance with National Heart Month.

All of this and more is the excitement of February! Watch students' smiles widen and their eyes brighten as they enter your "come alive" classroom. Your classroom will say "February is here!" from the ceiling to the floor, from windows and doors, from work sheets and activity projects, from stories and books, and especially from you — an enthusiastic, "project planned" teacher!

This little book of FEBRUARY PATTERNS, PROJECTS & PLANS has been put together with tender loving care to help you be prepared to meet every one of the school days in February with special treats, learning projects and fun surprises that will make your students eager to participate in every phase of the daily schedule and look forward to the next day. Best of all, the patterns, projects and plans are ready for quick and easy use and require no elaborate materials and very little advance preparation.

For your convenience, the materials in this book have been organized around five major unit themes. Each of the patterns, projects and plans can be used independently of the unit plan, however, to be just as effective in classrooms in which teachers choose not to use a unit approach. All are planned to complement and enrich adopted curriculum schemes and to meet young children's interests and learning needs.

Major unit themes include:

- Fabulous February!
- Follow The Directions, Please
- Valentine's Day
- Chinese New Year
- The Human Body Is A Marvelous Machine

Each unit includes a major objective and things to do; poster/booklet cover, bulletin board or display; patterns; art and/or an assembly project; reproducible basic skills activities; and book, story and poem suggestions to make the literature connection.

Other topics, special days and events for which patterns, projects and plans have been provided include:

- Groundhog Day (February 2)
- National Heart Month
- National Children's Dental Health Week (first week in February)
- Washington's & Lincoln's Birthdays

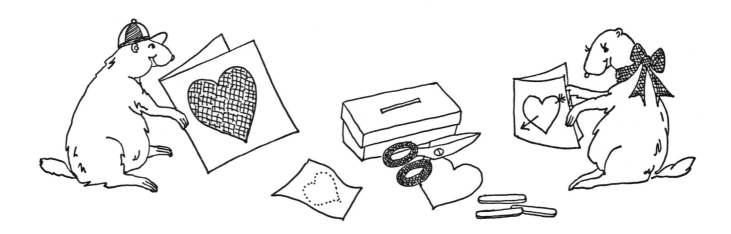

FABULOUS FEBRUARY

Major Objective:
Children will develop awareness of the colors, sights, sounds, special days and events that characterize the month of February.

Things To Do:

- Select and reproduce the awards, classroom helpers and work sheets from this book that are appropriate for your class and plan the order for their use. Let the children use the patterns throughout the book to make decorations for windows, desks, bulletin boards, and even doors and floors!

- Tell the class how early settlers from Germany believed the groundhog would come out of hibernation on February 2 to observe the weather. If the groundhog saw his shadow, he would go back into his hole and there would be more cold weather. If he did not see his shadow, he would climb out of his hole to enjoy the warm weather that was on the way. Check to see if the sun is shining on February 2 and let the class make a prediction for an early or late spring!

- Send the "letter to parents" (page 10) home to announce the month's plans and to ask for donations for your materials collection. Check your supplies to be sure you are ready for the month!

To complete the activities in this book, you will need:

construction paper (assorted colors)	popsicle sticks or tongue depressors
drawing paper	party items (see pgs. 29 & 30)
tissue paper (assorted colors)	articles made in China (see pg. 49)
crayons & markers	Chinese foods (optional - see pg. 49)
scissors	noise makers (see pg. 50)
paste	plastic drinking straws
tape	darning needle
stapler	heavy thread
pencils	ingredients for recipes (pgs. 31 & 58)
magazines & catalogs	stethoscope (see pg. 67)
shoe boxes	world map & globe

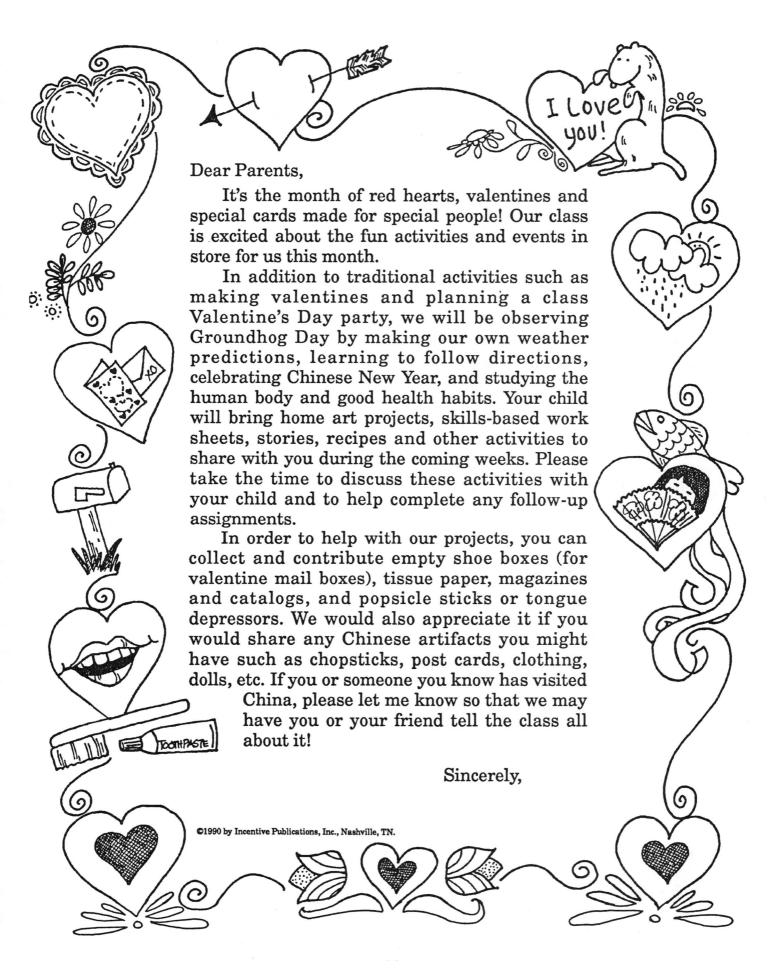

Dear Parents,

It's the month of red hearts, valentines and special cards made for special people! Our class is excited about the fun activities and events in store for us this month.

In addition to traditional activities such as making valentines and planning a class Valentine's Day party, we will be observing Groundhog Day by making our own weather predictions, learning to follow directions, celebrating Chinese New Year, and studying the human body and good health habits. Your child will bring home art projects, skills-based work sheets, stories, recipes and other activities to share with you during the coming weeks. Please take the time to discuss these activities with your child and to help complete any follow-up assignments.

In order to help with our projects, you can collect and contribute empty shoe boxes (for valentine mail boxes), tissue paper, magazines and catalogs, and popsicle sticks or tongue depressors. We would also appreciate it if you would share any Chinese artifacts you might have such as chopsticks, post cards, clothing, dolls, etc. If you or someone you know has visited China, please let me know so that we may have you or your friend tell the class all about it!

Sincerely,

©1990 by Incentive Publications, Inc., Nashville, TN.

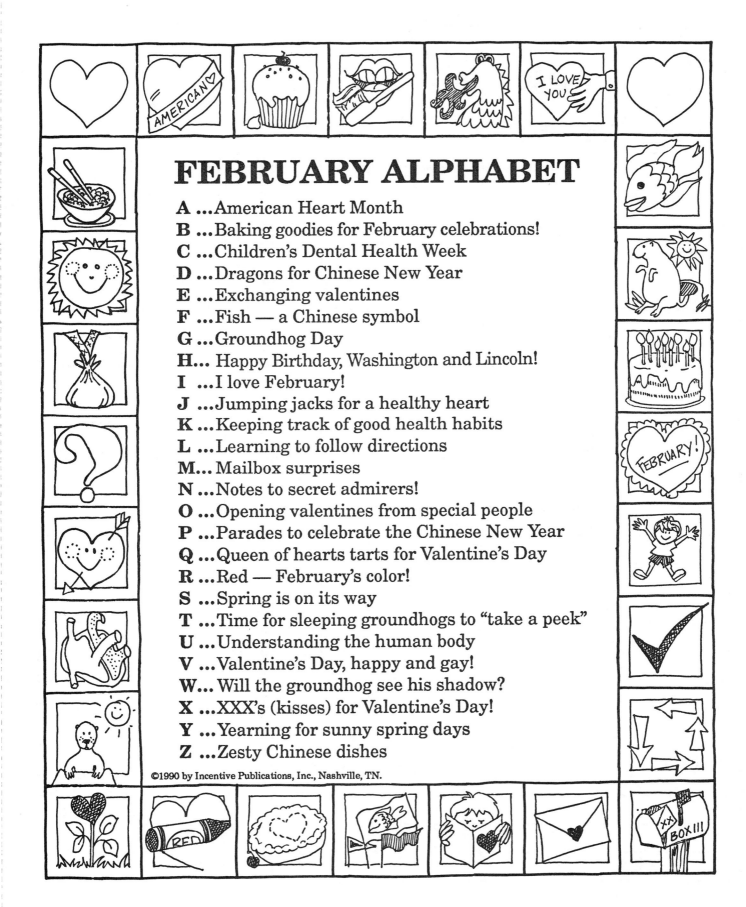

FEBRUARY ALPHABET

A ...American Heart Month
B ...Baking goodies for February celebrations!
C ...Children's Dental Health Week
D ...Dragons for Chinese New Year
E ...Exchanging valentines
F ...Fish — a Chinese symbol
G ...Groundhog Day
H... Happy Birthday, Washington and Lincoln!
I ...I love February!
J ...Jumping jacks for a healthy heart
K ...Keeping track of good health habits
L ...Learning to follow directions
M... Mailbox surprises
N ...Notes to secret admirers!
O ...Opening valentines from special people
P ...Parades to celebrate the Chinese New Year
Q ...Queen of hearts tarts for Valentine's Day
R ...Red — February's color!
S ...Spring is on its way
T ...Time for sleeping groundhogs to "take a peek"
U ...Understanding the human body
V ...Valentine's Day, happy and gay!
W... Will the groundhog see his shadow?
X ...XXX's (kisses) for Valentine's Day!
Y ...Yearning for sunny spring days
Z ...Zesty Chinese dishes

©1990 by Incentive Publications, Inc., Nashville, TN.

FEBRUARY MANAGEMENT CHART

© 1990 by Incentive Publications, Inc., Nashville, TN.

FEBRUARY

©1990 by Incentive Publications, Inc., Nashville, TN.

FEBRUARY

Sunday	Monday	Tuesday	Wednesday	Thursday	Friday	Saturday

©1990 by Incentive Publications, Inc., Nashville, TN.

HOW TO USE THE FEBRUARY CALENDAR

Use the calendar to:

... find on what day of the week the first day of February falls.
... count the number of days in February.
... find the number on the calendar which represents February.
... mark the birthdays of "February babies" in your room
... mark special days

- Groundhog Day (Feb. 2)
- National Children's Dental Health Week (First week in Feb.)
- Chinese New Year (Feb. 7)
- Abraham Lincoln's Birthday (Feb. 12)
- Valentine's Day (Feb. 14)
- George Washington's Birthday (Feb. 22 — legal holiday Feb. 20)

CALENDAR ART

©1990 by Incentive Publications, Inc., Nashville, TN.

CLASSROOM HELPERS

A LOVE NOTE

FROM YOUR TEACHER

Teacher's Helper

GOOD HEALTH AWARD

Name tag

©1990 by Incentive Publications, Inc., Nashville, TN.

FEBRUARY DOORKNOB
DECORATION

Color and cut out this doorknob decoration.
Hang it on your door to tell the world that Valentine's Day is near!

©1990 by Incentive Publications, Inc., Nashville, TN.

GROUNDHOG SHOW-OFF

To "show off" good work, help the children color and cut out groundhog show-offs to attach to their papers. Show-offs make attractive bulletin board displays and great "take homes"!

Attach paper here.

©1990 by Incentive Publications, Inc., Nashville, TN.

GROUNDHOG COMMUNICATORS

The good news is _____
_____ %
_____
_____
_____
_____ .

©1990 by Incentive Publications, Inc., Nashville, TN.

Just a reminder—

To: _____
_____
_____
_____

From: _____

Date: _____

©1990 by Incentive Publications, Inc., Nashville, TN.

Here's what's happening in our classroom

Week of _____

Monday _____

Tuesday _____

Wednesday _____

Thursday _____

Friday _____

©1990 by Incentive Publications, Inc., Nashville, TN.

FOLLOW THE DIRECTIONS, PLEASE

Major Objective:
Children will develop awareness of the importance of following directions and will gain experience in following both verbal and simple written directions.

Things To Do:

- Play games in which the players are asked to follow simple verbal directions such as *Mother May I, Simon Says, Hokey Pokey,* etc.

- Distribute sheets of drawing paper and crayons and ask the children to follow step-by-step verbal directions to complete a folding and drawing activity. Demonstrate how to fold the paper as you give the following directions.

    1. Fold the paper in half and then fold it in half again.

    2. Unfold the paper. You should have four "boxes."

    3. Number the boxes 1, 2, 3, and 4.

    4. Draw one heart in box 1, two hearts in box 2, three hearts in box 3, and four hearts in box 4.

    5. Color the hearts red.

- Direct the children to complete tasks using positional words. Begin with simple one-step procedures and move to more complicated directions.

    Example: Place a red crayon on the art table beside the red paint. Put a book under the teacher's desk. Hold your right hand over your head.

Then ask the children to take turns giving simple directions for others to follow. Ask them to watch carefully to see if the directions are carried out properly and to give the directions a second time if necessary.

- Ask one child at a time to follow verbal directions to perform a simple task.

    Example: Walk to the board. Pick up an eraser and a piece of chalk. Carry the eraser and chalk to the table and place them on the table.

Increase the number of steps required to perform the task as dictated by the child's performance.

- Provide old magazines and catalogs and give the children verbal directions for finding specific pictures.

   Example: Find one child, one pet and one building. Cut out the pictures and paste them on a sheet of drawing paper. Make up a story about the pictures.

- Have fun with stress-relieving activities designed to help the children learn to follow verbal directions for making creative body movements.

   Example: Stand tall, stretch your arms high and use your arms to make a circle over your head. Now let your arms fall to your sides. Touch your toes, your head and your tummy.

Or, play games such as Jungle Walk.

   Example: This is the way the elephant walks — thump, thump, thump (the children make trunks with their arms and swing from side to side as they walk). This is the way the tiger stalks — proud and fierce

(the children sneak across the floor, staring straight ahead). After playing the game several times, let the children supply other animals and actions!

- Reproduce pages 23 - 27 in quantities to meet the needs of the class. Have the children complete the dot-to-dot activity (page 23) and color the page for use as a booklet cover. Present one of the remaining pages each day. Collect the completed activities daily. When all of the activities have been completed, help the children staple the pages together to make "take home" booklets. (Note: Use the verbally-directed activities to reinforce concept and skill development. You may choose to send a note home with each child suggesting that some of the activities be used as "homework.") Reproduce page 28 for each child and help the children make stand-up groundhogs as a culminating activity.

- Use the activities from the other units in this book in teacher-directed settings.

WILL THE GROUNDHOG SEE A SHADOW?

Connect the dots from 1 to 20 to find a weather forecaster.

Name _____

Date _____

Following one-step directions to complete a dot-to-dot picture
©1990 by Incentive Publications, Inc., Nashville, TN.

MR. GROUNDHOG AND FRIENDS

Find and color 5 animals hiding in the picture
Color the animals.

Name _____

Date _____

Following two-step directions to find & color a hidden picture
©1990 by Incentive Publications, Inc., Nashville, TN.

A SUNNY DAY PICTURE

Color the sun yellow.
Color the groundhog brown.
Color the trees and grass green.

Name _____

Date _____

Following three-step directions to complete a picture
©1990 by Incentive Publications, Inc., Nashville, TN.

A FUNNY PICNIC

Draw wings on the bunny
Draw a hat on the raccoon.
Draw sunglasses on the groundhog.
Color the picture.

Name _____

Date _____

MATH TIME

1. Count the animals.
2. How many animals did you count? _____
3. Color the first animal brown.
4. Color the second animal black.
5. Color the third animal green.
6. Color the other animal any color you choose.

Name _____

Date _____

Using numerical sequence to complete directions
©1990 by Incentive Publications, Inc., Nashville, TN.

A GROUNDHOG STORY TO TELL

Color and cut out the groundhog.
Fold and stand up the groundhog.
Make up a story about the groundhog and his shadow.

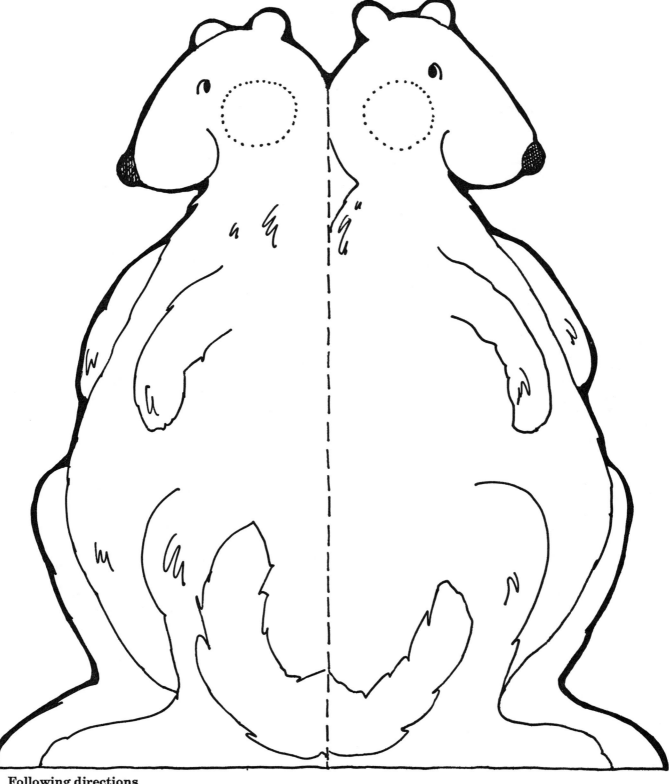

Following directions
©1990 by Incentive Publications, Inc., Nashville, TN.

VALENTINE'S DAY

Major Objective:
Children will develop appreciation of Valentine's Day as a holiday that symbolizes love and friendship and will become familiar with the history and symbols associated with the day.

Things To Do:

- To set the stage for Valentine's Day projects and activities, read and share *The Great Valentine's Day Balloon Race* (see page 78).

- Use the patterns on pages 33 - 35, 37, 43, 45 and 46 to make posters, cards, chains, borders, name tags, etc. to decorate the room from the ceiling to the floor! Be sure to make extras to share with the principal, secretary and cafeteria workers and to send home with the children during the month. After all, February is noted for being the month for sharing tokens of affection and appreciation!

- Have the children make special Valentine's Day cards for residents of a nursing home or a senior citizen's group. Reproduce the pattern on page 37 for each child. Help the children add their own decorations and messages. If possible, plan a class field trip to deliver the cards!

- Bake "Queen of Hearts Tarts" (see page 31) and send the recipe home with the children so that their families can make quick and easy tarts for Valentine's Day.

- Have the children bring shoe boxes or white bakery boxes from home to decorate for valentine mailboxes. Provide markers, scissors and red construction paper. Let the children use the patterns on pages 33, 34, 45 and 46 to decorate their boxes. Help the children cut "slits" in the tops of their boxes to complete their mailboxes!

- Reproduce pages 38 - 40 for each child. Help the children read and enjoy the rhymes. Ask the children to pick out the rhyming words and supply other rhyming words. Then let the children color the pictures, cut the pages apart and staple them together to make "Valentine Rhyme Books" to take home and share with their families.

- Involve the children in planning a fabulous, no-fail Valentine's Day party. Remember to plan simple games, activities and refreshments that will be easy to prepare, present and clean up. Providing white cups, napkins and plates for the children to decorate serves two purposes — the children spend "party time" involved in a satisfying activity and they have one-of-a-kind finished products which they can "show off" and use. Make party hats (see page 36) and valentine mailboxes (see page 29) before the party and have them ready for the big day!

- Reproduce page 46 for each child. Have the children cut out the hearts. Provide sheets of red construction paper and paste and instruct the children to arrange the hearts on the paper to make valentine collages. Encourage the children to move the hearts around on the page to make various designs before pasting them in place. Display the collages on a bulletin board until Valentine's Day and then send them home with the children.

- Read and discuss Joan Walsh Anglund's *Love Is A Special Way Of Feeling, What Color Is Love?* and *A Friend Is Someone Who Likes You* as motivation for a discussion about friendship. Ask the children to discuss characteristics of a good friend and to name classmates who exhibit "friendly traits." Create a chart with the title "A Good Friend Is..." and list the traits of a good friend as the children name them.

- Have the children make Valentine's Day cards for parents or grandparents (see page 43). Help the children address the cards and then take a field trip to the post office to mail the valentines. Allow each child to drop his or her card in the mailbox. If possible, arrange in advance for a postal employee to tell the class about the postal system and take the class on a tour of the post office. If a field trip is not possible, walk as a group to the nearest mailbox and drop off the cards.

THE QUEEN OF HEARTS

The Queen of Hearts
    She made some tarts,
All on a summer's day.

The Knave of Hearts,
    He stole the tarts,
And took them clean away.

The King of Hearts,
    Called for the tarts,
And beat the Knave full sore.

The Knave of Hearts
    Brought back the tarts,
And vow'd he'd steal no more.

Queen of Hearts Tarts

What To Use:
2 cans of biscuits
1 jar of strawberry or cherry jam
2 non-stick muffin tins
pot holder
teaspoon

What To Do:
1. Divide the biscuits in half.
2. Roll the biscuit halves into small balls. Press each ball into a muffin cup and spread the ball around the sides.
3. Bake 10 minutes at 350 degrees.
4. Remove from oven and cool.
5. Spoon jam inside each tart.

©1990 by Incentive Publications, Inc., Nashville, TN.

Construction:

1. Reproduce the patterns on pages 33 - 35. Enlarge the Valentine's Day banner and color it with markers. Cut two cupids out of construction paper and/or color them with markers.
2. Have each child cut a heart out of red construction paper. Instruct the children to write their names and draw pictures of themselves on their hearts.
3. Assemble the board as shown above.

Variations:

- *With All Our Hearts We Love Mother Goose:* Draw or paste pictures of characters from favorite Mother Goose rhymes on the hearts.
- *With All Our Hearts We Love Good Work:* Attach the children's good work to the hearts.
- Use the Valentine's Day banner as a door or hall decoration.

HEART

©1990 by Incentive Publications, Inc., Nashville, TN.

CUPID

©1990 by Incentive Publications, Inc., Nashville, TN.

VALENTINE'S DAY BANNER

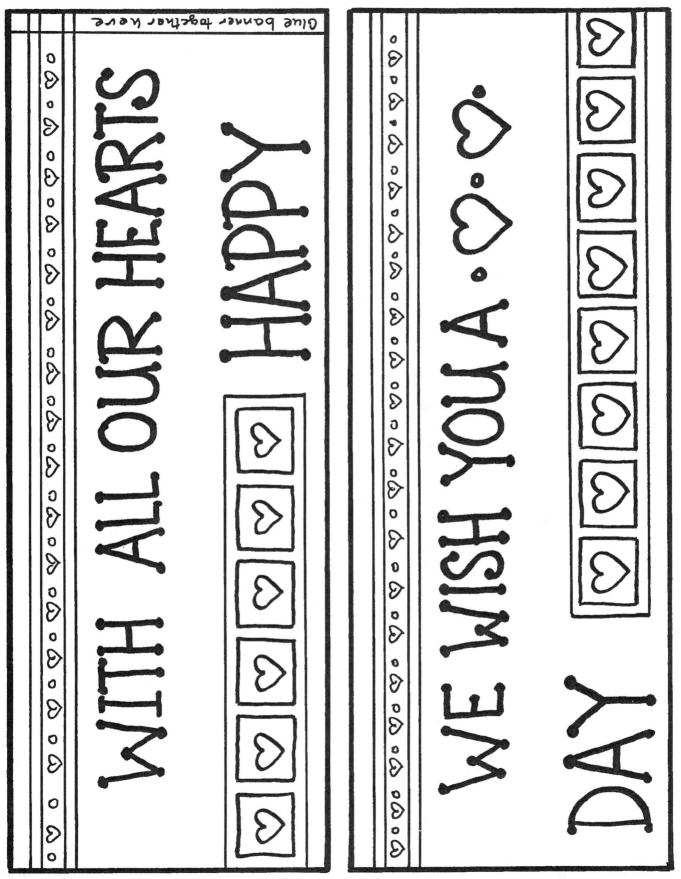

Glue banner together here

WITH ALL OUR HEARTS HAPPY

WE WISH YOU A ♥•♥•♥

DAY

©1990 by Incentive Publications, Inc., Nashville, TN.

VALENTINE'S DAY PARTY HATS

Have the children make party hats a day or two before your Valentine's Day celebration. Let the children wear their hats all day long on party day!

What To Use:
12" x 18" red construction paper
   (1 sheet for each child)
pink and white construction paper
scissors

paste
markers
stapler

What To Do:

1. Instruct each child to fold and crease a two-inch strip of a 12" x 18" sheet of red construction paper to form a brim for the hat.

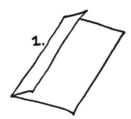

2. Direct the children to fold their papers into cone shapes as shown.

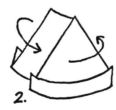

3. Help the children staple their cones together to form hats.

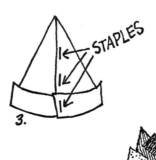

4. Have the children write their names on the brims of their hats with markers.

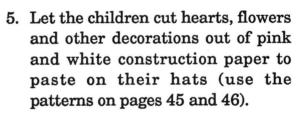

5. Let the children cut hearts, flowers and other decorations out of pink and white construction paper to paste on their hats (use the patterns on pages 45 and 46).

POP-UP
VALENTINE CARD

1. Cut out the card.
2. Fold along the dotted lines.
3. Color the heart red.
4. Write a message inside the card and decorate the card with crayons or markers.

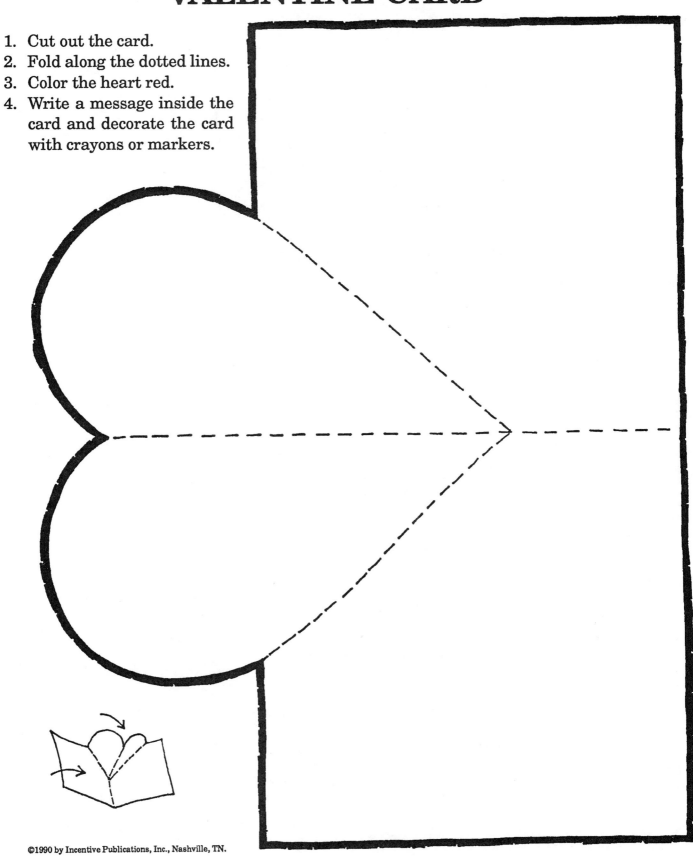

©1990 by Incentive Publications, Inc., Nashville, TN.

My Book Of Valentine Rhymes

By _____   Date _____

©1990 by Incentive Publications, Inc., Nashville, TN.

Valentine, Valentine,

Valentine so fine,

Valentine, Valentine,

Will you be mine?

©1990 by Incentive Publications, Inc., Nashville, TN.

Bears love honey,

Flowers love dew,

Bankers love money

And I love you.

©1990 by Incentive Publications, Inc., Nashville, TN.

The ocean is deep,

It's wide and blue.

My love for you

Is steady and true.

©1990 by Incentive Publications, Inc., Nashville, TN.

If I were King

Know what I'd do?

I'd buy a fine ring

And give it to you!

©1990 by Incentive Publications, Inc., Nashville, TN.

Roses are red,

Violets are blue.

Sugar is sweet

And so are you!

©1990 by Incentive Publications, Inc., Nashville, TN.

Name _____

HEARTS TO REMEMBER

Fold the page in half along
    the dotted lines.
Look carefully at the
    picture below.
Now turn the page over.

Draw the picture as you
    remember it.
No peeking!

Following directions to use recall skills
©1990 by Incentive Publications, Inc., Nashville, TN.

Name _____

A VALENTINE TO MAIL

Cut out the pictures below and paste them in the correct boxes to tell a story.

Sequencing

©1990 by Incentive Publications, Inc., Nashville, TN.

A VALENTINE FOR
SOMEONE SPECIAL

Make a valentine card for someone you love.
Address the card and mail it!

cut

fold

Stamp

_____

_____

_____

©1990 by Incentive Publications, Inc., Nashville, TN.

Name _____

PARTY TIME

Mark the path to help Chippy Chipmunk find her way to the Valentine's Day party.

Visual discrimination/working a maze
©1990 by Incentive Publications, Inc., Nashville, TN.

VALENTINE'S DAY PATTERNS

BE MY Valentine!

Happy Valentine's Day!

©1990 by Incentive Publications, Inc., Nashville, TN.

HEARTS, HEARTS, HEARTS

©1990 by Incentive Publications, Inc., Nashville, TN.

THE POSTAL SYSTEM

©1990 by Incentive Publications, Inc., Nashville, TN.

Name _____

BROKEN HEARTS

Cut out the heart halves.
Paste each heart half in the correct space.
Say the numerals.

CHINESE NEW YEAR

Major Objective:
Children will develop understanding of a major holiday celebrated by people in another country and will learn about the customs, colors and festivities of the Chinese New Year celebration.

Things To Do:

- To develop readiness for this unit, reproduce the "Chinese New Year" story (page 51) for each child. Read the story aloud and discuss the holiday with the children. Have the children color the border and take the story home to share with family members.

- Help the children locate China on a world map and a globe. Lead a discussion about the major cities and attractions of China and China's neighboring countries. Take care not to lead the discussion beyond the children's level of understanding. If possible, invite someone who has visited China to talk to the children about his or her travels.

- Lead a discussion of the similarities and differences of the Chinese New Year celebration and the New Year celebration in your community.

- Let the children help to plan a Dim-Sun meal. Explain that a Dim-Sun is a favorite meal of the Chinese people which is made up of small portions of different kinds of foods. Explain that each food is brought to the table one at a time and passed around the table. You may want to serve fried rice, Chinese noodles, bean sprouts, Chinese tea and fortune cookies at your Dim-Sun! If there is a Chinese restaurant in your neighborhood, try to secure a menu and chopsticks! As a follow-up activity, reproduce page 59 and help the children make their own paper fortune cookies.

- Display articles "made in China" (clothing, fans, cards, stamps, dolls, dishes, etc.) on a sharing table. Ask the children to bring articles from home to contribute to the display. Cut pictures out of magazines and travel brochures and add these to the collection.

- Red is the color most used in decorations and favors for the Chinese New Year. Have a red day in your classroom. Ask the children to wear red clothes and to bring one red toy, book or food to share with the class. Have the children name as many red things as they can and list these items on a large chart. Help the children look for pictures of red things in magazines and catalogs and add the pictures to the chart. Once you get started, the children will add their own suggestions and ideas.

- Plan a Chinese New Year parade. Have the children make chains, fans, scrolls, banners, streamers and signs to use as decorations

to carry in the parade (see pages 52 - 57). Let the children use rhythm band instruments, pots and pans, horns and other noise-makers as they parade. (If you have enough noisemakers, you may need to stage the parade outside!)

- Discuss how the Chinese order years in cycles of twelve and name each cycle for a particular animal. Share the legend of how Buddha invited all of the animals to a big celebration to which only twelve went. Buddha supposedly named a year after each animal that attended the celebration. Reproduce and distribute page 66 and help the children identify and discuss each animal. The children may color the animals and take the page home for further discussion.

- Read *Gung Hay Fat Choy* (see page 78) to explain the significance of the Chinese New Year.

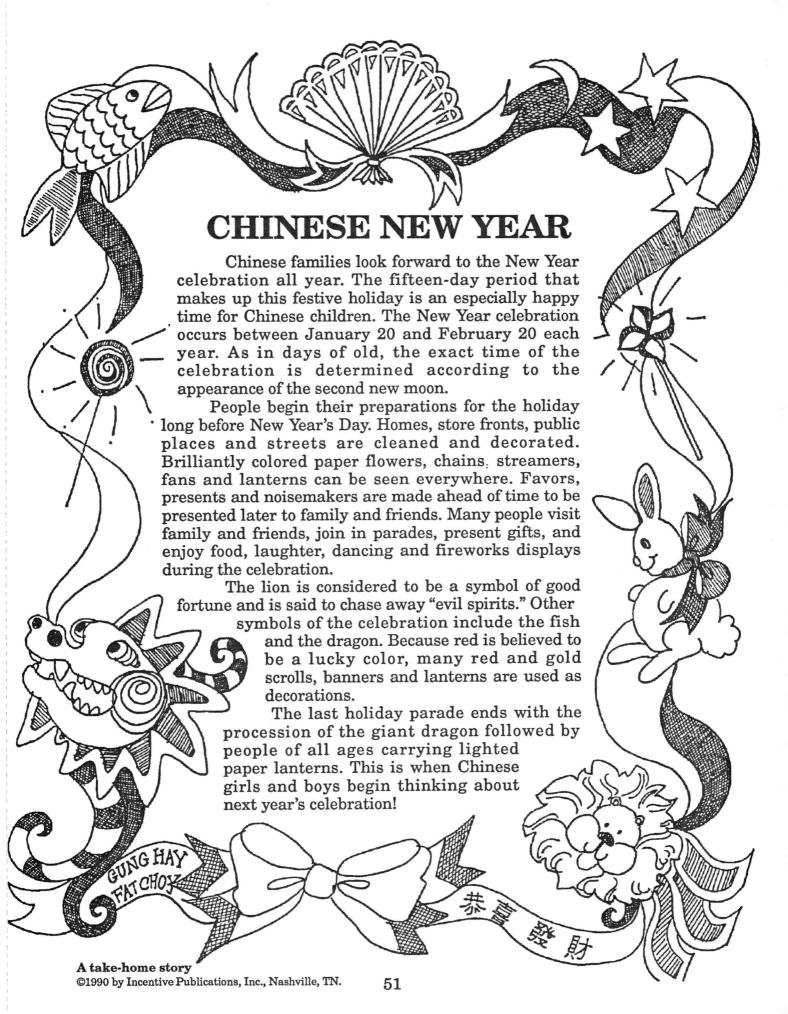

CHINESE NEW YEAR

Chinese families look forward to the New Year celebration all year. The fifteen-day period that makes up this festive holiday is an especially happy time for Chinese children. The New Year celebration occurs between January 20 and February 20 each year. As in days of old, the exact time of the celebration is determined according to the appearance of the second new moon.

People begin their preparations for the holiday long before New Year's Day. Homes, store fronts, public places and streets are cleaned and decorated. Brilliantly colored paper flowers, chains, streamers, fans and lanterns can be seen everywhere. Favors, presents and noisemakers are made ahead of time to be presented later to family and friends. Many people visit family and friends, join in parades, present gifts, and enjoy food, laughter, dancing and fireworks displays during the celebration.

The lion is considered to be a symbol of good fortune and is said to chase away "evil spirits." Other symbols of the celebration include the fish and the dragon. Because red is believed to be a lucky color, many red and gold scrolls, banners and lanterns are used as decorations.

The last holiday parade ends with the procession of the giant dragon followed by people of all ages carrying lighted paper lanterns. This is when Chinese girls and boys begin thinking about next year's celebration!

GUNG HAY FAT CHOY

恭喜發財

A take-home story
©1990 by Incentive Publications, Inc., Nashville, TN.

CHINESE CHARACTER FANS

Let the children make Chinese character fans to use in a class New Year parade!

What To Use:
construction paper (2 sheets for each child)   scissors
popsicle sticks or tongue depressors (1 for each child)   paste
tag board

What To Do:
1. Reproduce the patterns on pages 53 - 55. Cut them out and trace around them on tag board to make durable patterns for the children to use.
2. Provide each child with two sheets of construction paper, paste, scissors and a popsicle stick or tongue depressor.
3. Help each child cut two dragons, two lions or two fish patterns out of construction paper. (Have 1/3 of the class make dragons, 1/3 make lions and 1/3 make fish.)
4. Let the children use crayons or markers to decorate their patterns to make a "front" and a "back" side.
5. Instruct the children to paste a popsicle stick or tongue depressor between the front and back sides to make a handle for the fan.
6. Let the children wave their fans in a class New Year parade!

FISH PATTERN

©1990 by Incentive Publications, Inc., Nashville, TN.

DRAGON PATTERN

©1990 by Incentive Publications, Inc., Nashville, TN.

LION PATTERN

©1990 by Incentive Publications, Inc., Nashville, TN.

BUTTERFLIES, BIRDS, BEES AND FLOWERS TO CELEBRATE THE CHINESE NEW YEAR

What To Use:
plastic drinking straws
colored tissue paper
   (as many colors as possible)
darning needle
heavy thread

What To Do:
1. Have the children cut fanciful shapes out of bright colors of tissue paper (use the patterns on page 57 and have the children cut free-form shapes, too). Instruct the children to cut on the fold to make "double shapes" — this will give body to the chain.
2. Cut drinking straws into one and two-inch lengths. The different lengths will add interest to the chain.
3. Thread a darning needle with a long, heavy thread and tie a knot at the end of the thread.
4. Help one child at a time push the needle through a paper shape and then through a section of straw. Continue alternating shapes and straws in this manner until the chain is of the desired length.
5. Tie a knot in the end of the thread to secure the chain.

Suggestion: Hang the children's chains, along with other decorations, on windows, doors and bulletin boards!

56

BUTTERFLIES, BIRDS, BEES AND FLOWERS

©1990 by Incentive Publications, Inc., Nashville, TN.

RECIPES FOR THE CHINESE NEW YEAR CELEBRATION

Egg Drop Soup

What To Use:
6 cups chicken broth
1 1/2 cups cooked rice or fine noodles
4 eggs
4 tbs. lemon juice

What To Do:
1. Heat chicken broth and cooked rice or noodles to a rolling boil.
2. Beat eggs and lemon juice in a large bowl just long enough to combine.
3. Gradually pour the hot broth over the eggs, stirring constantly so as not to curdle the eggs but to allow them to shred.
4. Serve at once in paper cups.
   Makes 12 servings.

©1990 by Incentive Publications, Inc., Nashville, TN.

Chinese Fried Rice

What To Use:
3 tbs. vegetable oil
6 green onions, thinly sliced
1 pkg. frozen green peas
2 eggs, beaten

2 tbs. soy sauce
1/2 tsp. sugar
4 cups cooked rice (cold)
salt & pepper, if desired

What To Do:
1. Heat oil in skillet over medium heat.
2. Stir in onion and cook for 2 minutes. Add peas and heat.
3. Stir in rice. Coat with oil and pea mixture. Fry for 2 - 3 minutes.
4. Pour beaten eggs over rice. Cook, stirring often until egg is set.
5. Mix soy sauce and sugar. Add to rice and stir.
6. Season with salt and pepper if desired.

©1990 by Incentive Publications, Inc., Nashville, TN.

CHINESE FORTUNE COOKIES

1. Cut out the fortune cookies below.
2. Fold each cookie along the dotted line.
3. Paste the edges together, leaving a small opening at the top.
4. Write or draw "messages" on each fortune strip.
5. Cut out the messages and slip one inside each cookie.

Give the fortune cookies to someone in your family!

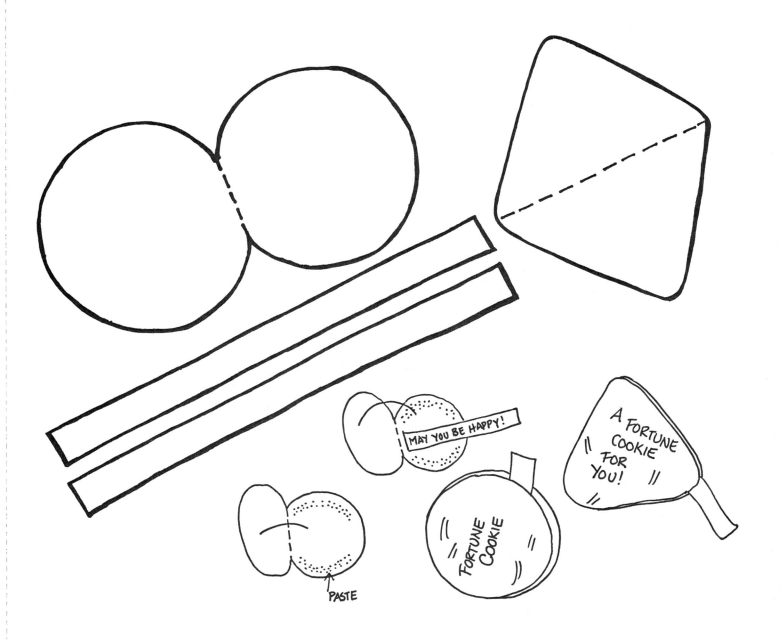

©1990 by Incentive Publications, Inc., Nashville, TN

Name _____

ALPHABET SEARCH

All 26 letters of the alphabet are hiding in this Chinese New Year's Day parade.

Find and color the 26 letters.

Recognizing letters of the alphabet
©1990 by Incentive Publications, Inc., Nashville, TN.

Construction:

1. Cover the board with red construction paper or butcher paper.
2. Reproduce the border patterns on page 64 and cut them out of gold paper.
3. Cut the caption "Chinese New Year" out of gold paper (enlarge and use the letter patterns on pages 62 and 63).
4. Reproduce the fish, dragon and lion patterns on pages 53 - 55 and color them with markers or cut them out of bright colors of construction paper.
5. Reproduce the animal patterns on page 66. Help the children cut the animals out of bright colors of construction paper.
6. Assemble the board as shown.
7. Display the children's drawings, work sheets and projects on the board.

Note: Since golden coins are given to children as part of the New Year celebration, cut coins out of gold paper scraps and add them to the board. Artifacts such as chopsticks, fans, etc. also may be added if they are available.

FEBRUARY
ALPHABET

©1990 by Incentive Publications, Inc., Nashville, TN.

©1990 by Incentive Publications, Inc., Nashville, TN.

CHINESE PAPER BORDERS

Accordion fold strips of gold foil to match the size of the pattern
Trace a pattern onto paper and cut.
Be sure dotted lines touch edges.

©1990 by Incentive Publications, Inc., Nashville, TN.

CHINESE NEW YEAR PATTERNS

©1990 by Incentive Publications, Inc., Nashville, TN.

SYMBOLS
FOR THE CHINESE NEW YEAR

©1990 by Incentive Publications, Inc., Nashville, TN.

THE HUMAN BODY IS A MARVELOUS MACHINE

Major Objective:
Children will develop appreciation of the uniqueness of the human body, will gain awareness of the parts of the body and the changes taking place in their own bodies, and will develop responsibility for the proper care of their bodies.

Things To Do:

- Discuss the human body and ask the children to identify and discuss various body parts. Explain that all bodies are constantly growing and changing. Ask each child to think of things that he or she can or cannot do this year that he or she could or could not do last year because of these changes.

    Example: I can reach the top shelf of my bookcase because my legs are longer; I cannot ride my tricycle anymore because my legs are too long.

    Reproduce page 68 for each child and have the children complete the work sheet. Add the work sheets to a bulletin board display.

- Cut pictures of people of all ages engaged in various activities out of magazines and catalogs. Paste the pictures on sheets of construction paper and staple the sheets together to form a book. Place the book on a reading table and let the children thumb through the book during free time and discuss the differences in the people pictured.

- Enlarge the skeleton on page 69 and display it on a chart or bulletin board. Explain that this is a picture of the bones of a human being. Discuss the word skeleton and help the children understand its meaning.

- Since February is American Heart Month, discuss how the heart works and what things can be done to keep the heart healthy. Discuss the need for proper diet, exercise, rest etc. Let the children use a stethoscope to listen to their heartbeats as they sit, run, walk, jump, etc.

- Observe Children's Dental Health Week (first week in February) by asking a dental hygienist to visit the class to talk about proper dental hygiene. Use page 72 as a follow-up activity.

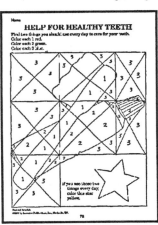

- As a culminating activity for this unit, reproduce page 76 for each child and ask the children to take the chart home and keep track of their health habits for one week.

Name _____

ME THEN AND NOW

This is the way I looked
when I was a baby.

This is the way I look now.

Awareness of changes in the human body
©1990 by Incentive Publications, Inc., Nashville, TN.

HUMAN SKELETON

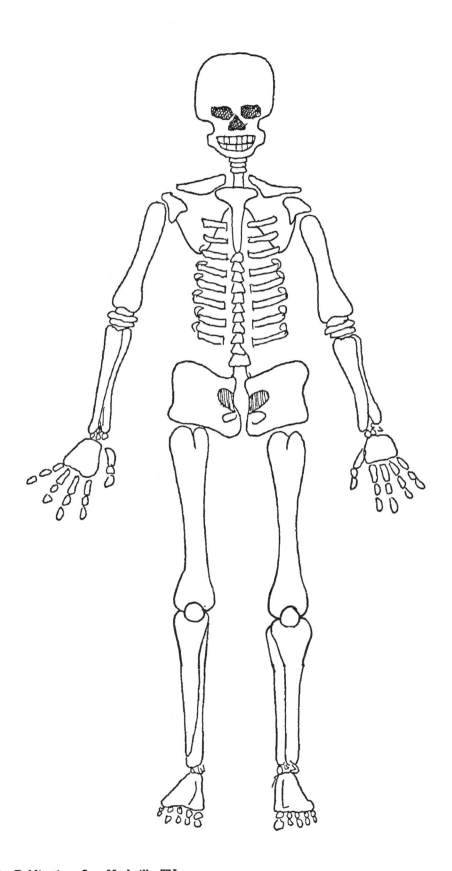

©1990 by Incentive Publications, Inc., Nashville, TN.

Name _____

HEARTBEAT

When you think of a heart, you probably often think of something that
    looks like a valentine.
The human heart is a muscle that pumps blood through the body.
Each time this muscle pumps, your heart beats.

This is a heart.

This is the way the human heart
    looks.

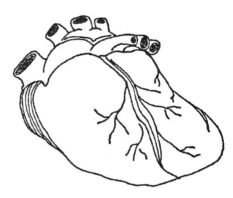

Draw a picture of yourself exercising to keep your heart healthy.

Understanding the human heart
©1990 by Incentive Publications, Inc., Nashville, TN.

Name _____

HOW HEALTHY ARE YOU?

The pictures below show good health habits.
Color the pictures of things that you do regularly.
Circle the other pictures.

Recognizing good health habits
©1990 by Incentive Publications, Inc., Nashville, TN.

HELP FOR HEALTHY TEETH

Find two things you should use every day to care for your teeth.
Color each 1 red.
Color each 2 green.
Color each 3 blue.

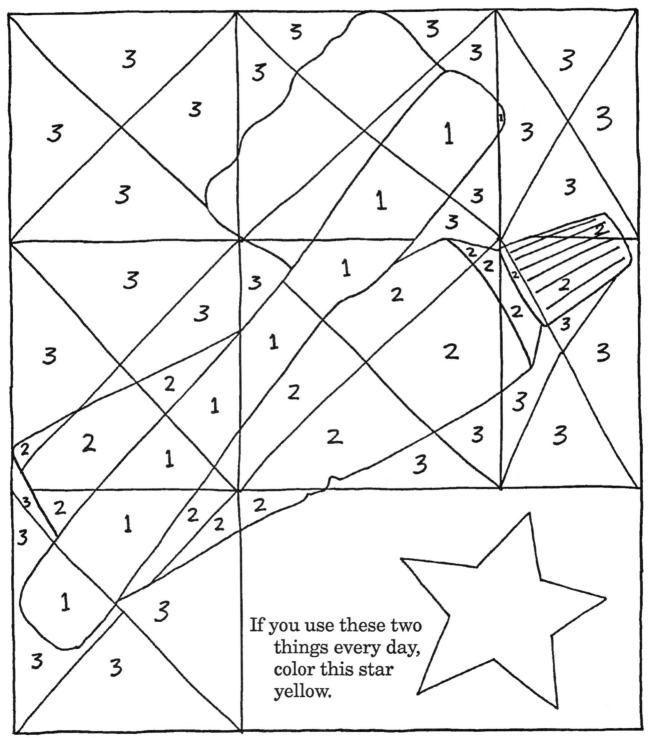

If you use these two things every day, color this star yellow.

Dental health
©1990 by Incentive Publications, Inc., Nashville, TN.

THINGS TO DO TO
HAVE HEALTHY TEETH

1. Brush

2. Floss

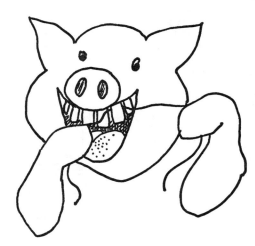

3. Eat right!

©1990 by Incentive Publications, Inc., Nashville, TN.

Name _____

HEALTHY FOODS

Color the picture of the healthier food in each box.
Make an X on the other food.

DRESSED FOR THE WEATHER

Wearing the right clothes for the weather helps us to stay healthy.
Draw a picture of yourself dressed for the weather shown in each box below.

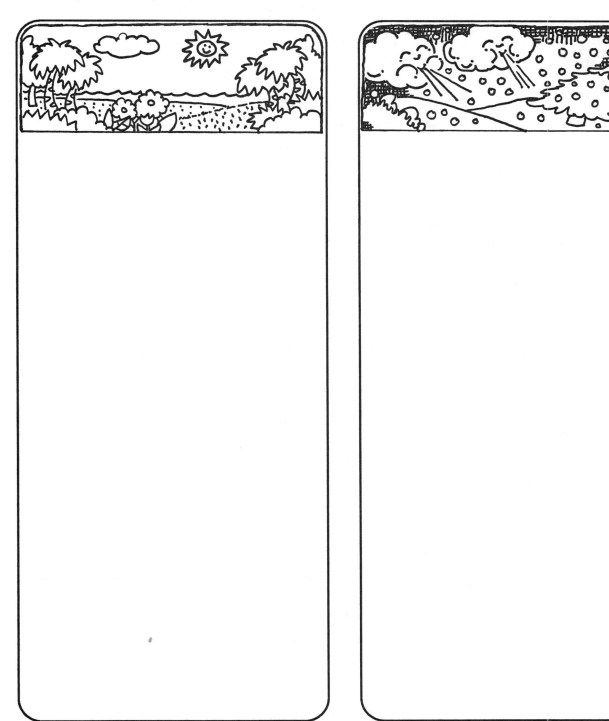

Awareness of appropriate dress
©1990 by Incentive Publications, Inc., Nashville, TN.

EXERCISE

©1990 by Incentive Publications, Inc., Nashville, TN.

MY HEALTH CHECK-UP

Name _____

Week of _____

	Sun.	Mon.	Tues.	Wed.	Thurs.	Fri.	Sat.
Sleep 8 or more hours							
Eat healthy foods							
Avoid sweets							
Exercise							
Brush teeth							
Bathe carefully							
Wash hands often							
Brush hair							
Dress for the weather							

Awareness of good health habits
©1990 by Incentive Publications, Inc., Nashville, TN.

BIBLIOGRAPHY

Alexander And The Terrible, Horrible, No Good, Very Bad Day. Judith Viorst. Atheneum.
As the children identify with Alexander on this day in his life when absolutely nothing goes right, they will feel just a little bit better about themselves and their own problems.

Baby Animals. Margaret Wise Brown. Random House.
The daily activities of some delightful young animals and a little girl who lives on a farm are shared in this beautiful picture book.

The Boy With Two Shadows. Margaret Mahy. J. B. Lippincott.
A young boy who agrees to take care of a witch's shadow while she is on vacation finds that having two shadows creates unexpected problems.

Caps, Hats, Socks And Mittens. Louise Borden. Scholastic, Inc.
From the caps, hats, socks, mittens and steaming cocoa of winter to the oranges and golds of the harvest season, this book humorously presents the seasonal images with which children identify.

Following Directions. Imogene Forte. Incentive Publications, Inc.
A mini-collection of quick-and-easy activities to help children learn to follow directions necessary for early learning success.

The Great Valentine's Day Balloon Race. Adrienne Adams. Charles Scribner's Sons.
This delightful story about two friends who make a balloon and enter the Valentine's Day race will delight young children.

Gung Hay Fat Choy. June Behrens. Children's Press.
Simple text and colorful photographs explain the significance of the Chinese New Year and describe its celebrations by Chinese Americans.

Let's Eat. True Kelly. E. P. Dutton, Inc.
Scrumptious illustrations and cleverly conceived headings make this a mouth-watering look at food, food sources, and good manners.

Little Love Story. Fernando Krahn. J. B. Lippincott Co.
Getting to the heart of a valentine gift, although it is quite complicated, proves to be worth the trouble.

The Missing Tarts. B. G. Hennessy. Viking Penguin.
When the Queen of Hearts discovers that her strawberry tarts have been stolen, she enlists the help of many popular nursery rhyme characters.

Poetry For Winter. Selected by Leland B. Jacobs. Garrard.
A wonderful collection of poems about winter wonders, winter animals and birds, winter play, winter holidays, and the end of winter.

The Scare Bird. Sid Fleischman. Greenwillow Books.
Beautiful paintings enhance this story about friendship that warms the heart. A lonesome little boy plays checkers with his scarecrow until a young farmhand comes along to relieve his loneliness.

Index